poems from the sangamon

poems from the sangamon

POEMS BY JOHN KNOEPFLE

UNIVERSITY OF ILLINOIS PRESS *Urbana and Chicago*

Publication of this work was supported in part by a grant from the National Endowment for the Arts.

This book is printed on acid-free paper.

Library of Congress Cataloging in Publication Data

Knoepfle, John.
  Poems from the Sangamon.

  1. Illinois—Poetry. I. Title
PS3561.N6P6 1985   811'.54   85-1133
ISBN 0-252-01243-7 (alk. paper)

Some of the poems in this book have appeared previously in the following publications:

"salt creek, kickapoo winter story," *ACM* (Fall 1985).

"circuit preacher, lines after cartwright," *Barnwood* 2 (Summer 1982).

"sandalwood poems" and "primroses and meadowlark eggs," *A Box of Sandalwood: Love Poems* (LaCrosse, Wis.: Juniper Press, 1979).

"mano," *The Chariton Review* (Fall 1978).

"farm auction," *Five Missouri Poets* (Kirksville, Mo.: Chariton Review Press, 1979).

"valentines day" (as "snow shadowing blue"), "back county musician," no. 3 from "in the country," (as "he plays for himself"), "he says if he hums," no. 2 from "in the country," "presidential election with blackbirds and swallows" (as "rain drying up in the fields"), and "man in overalls" (as "abstractions of the man"), *Focus Midwest* 14:86 (1980).

"another nile for pharaoh" and "ww II veteran," *New Letters* (Fall 1983).

"concert at normal," *Northeast* (Winter 1981–82).

"kickapoo burial, remembrance south of ellsworth," *The Pikestaff Forum* (Fall 1985) (as "kickapoo burial, remembrance south of ellsworth, illinois").

"it has to be any yes," "beneath the clocks at mason city thinking of the neutron bomb" (from two poems, "concrete twelve feet" and "rabbit without a foot"), "memorial day camp butler" (as "time to commemorate"), *Poems for the Hours* (Menomonie, Wis.: Uzzano Press, 1979).

"lines for the tribe of ben ishmael" and "at the sangamon headwaters," *River Styx* (Summer 1985).

"fisher woods in spring," "lick creek my own branch," and "year of the deep snow," *Spoon River Quarterly* (Summer 1981).

"self made in bloomington," *Spoon River Quarterly* (Spring 1983).

"lunch room, new berlin," "decatur," "soundings in glacial drift," "lincoln tomb, a report," "late winter in menard county," "bath," "poem for scott lucas," and "confluence," *Spoon River Quarterly* (Spring 1985).

"princess candidate, sangamon county fair," *This Awkward Mud* (published for Read Illinois, 1984).

"snowflakes and recorders" (as "lindsays house on a cold") and "owl in the capitol dome" (as "a man his time"), *The Village Magazine* (1979).

"after sundown" (as "on the front porch"), *Whetstone* (Kansas City, Mo.: BkMk Press, 1972).

acknowledgments

"marquette in winter camp . . . 1675" is shaped from the translation of
his letter in Joseph P. Donnelly, *Jacques Marquette, S.J., 1637–1675*.
Material for "kickapoo burial" and for subsequent poems with Kickapoo
motifs is derived in large part from Felipe and Dolores Latorre, *The Mexican
Kickapoo Indians*. Phrasing for much of "old settlers day, buckles grove,"
"year of the deep snow," and "kickapoo dance" has been borrowed from
Old Times in McLean County. "peter cartwrights dream" is a found poem
lined from the *Autobiography of Peter Cartwright, the Backwoods Preacher*,
and the phrasing for "circuit preacher, lines after cartwright" comes from
that book also. "clinton" has elements from Lincoln's "stands right" speech,
July 27, 1858, which is bronzed on the city square; there is also a moment
from David Etter's "Light in August," in *The Last Train to Prophetstown*.
"lincoln tomb, a report" quotes from the Second Inaugural Address and
Lincoln's comment on it in the letter to Thurlow Weed, both from Volume
VIII, *The Collected Works*. "lines for the tribe of ben ishmael" is in
heavy debt to Hugo P. Leaming, "The Ben Ishmael Tribe: A Fugitive 'Nation'
of the Old Northwest," in *The Ethnic Frontier*. The princess in "princess
candidate, sangamon county fair" makes use of thoughts from four
dispatches to the *Daily Pantagraph*, Mar. 19, 20, 20, and 22, 1925, printed
in Volume I, *The Papers of Adlai E. Stevenson*. "bath" is worked from
studies by Sandra Martin, "Sketches of a Town Called Bath" in the Mar.
24–30, 1983, edition of *Illinois Times*, and Jerry Klein in *Played in Peoria*.

I am grateful for the grant from the National Endowment for the Arts which
helped make possible the travel and research necessary for the completion
of *Poems from the Sangamon*.

and again for peg

contents

it has to be any yes *xv*

it has to be any yes
the pain of ice crystals
the woman bleeding
the little town
a water tower brooding
what does a man do
turning away
from the lines in his face
arrogance
a broken board
a door covered with snow

one

east in mclean county

this is a country of moraines
old prairie could have
gone on forever

mounds timbers points
groves islands savannas
a language of prairies

farmhouses on the high places
barns outbuildings
washed in the clear air

corn fields and soybean
enough for everyone

east of ellsworth
an osage orange hedge
stiffens the curve of the earth

four crows carry the sky away cawing

at the sangamon headwaters

culvert has a turtle in it
snapper with a thick neck
they get old
he has a grim smile
like someone who has been around a long time
who admires his enemies
and distrusts any friends
he has a tyrannosaur back
and a heart for his hide
he is a survivor it is no wonder
he stands for the earth
he is the wise one he knows
which way the river runs

saturday morning

it is as if you were walking
the top of creation
or you could jog these moraines forever
the river is ditched here
an interrupted line on the map
still green to the eye though
and crowding its slender grasses
the old channel
insinuates itself through cornfields
loops across and back
or coils alongside the ditch
still roaming its old valley
telephone cables overhead
catch the gusts of a storm
the gray light of morning whines
you turn searching for something
that should be there

representations of the self

1

he honors the wolf
and the skin of the wolf
he blesses the muzzle of the bear
he turns its dead eyes to the east
and rubs tobacco
in the muzzle of the bear

2

lay down your sorrow
my back hurts
cast your skin aside old snake
let me curl in the sun
the strong warm light of
midmorning the warm rocks of morning
my arthritic hands
their weak offerings
how could they please

3

sometimes when the sky
overwhelms the world crimson
a man becomes the image of himself
or at night when the horizon
rings him around with stars
he vanishes at the earths center

marquette in winter camp, chicago river, 1675

I know one of two things
god will break me
because I have been afraid
or he will give me his cross
which I have not borne
since I came to this country

the blessed immaculate virgin
will beg this for me
or god will speak my death
and I will stop offending him

I try to be ready
putting myself in his hands

pray for me and pray god
will keep me grateful
he has spoiled me always
with so many favors

beneath our tamaroa starlight

and the iroquois matched them
campfire for campfire
down the illinois river
on the opposite bank
until they backed on the mississippi
and that was the end

the old men with eyes
like stops for flutes
the children and the unborn
who clung so fiercely to the raw
rim of the world
the women who danced for us
like fireflies in the meadows
on the long good evenings

they went into darkness
the dawn could not rise from
they could not answer
their names when we called them

tamaroa prayer

let those who live with you
in your home in that other world
honor what they call you

let them listen to you
when you come to light your fire
and we will kindle our fires
as the year rounds in green corn

give us enough to eat
when the winter starves us
even the inside bark of the white oak
would nourish us

do not remember how we forget you
and our enemies we will forget them
thinking of you

come out of your house
and stay with us in summer
or we will be spoiled
in the months of plenty
and you will be angry with us

walk with your arm around us
as if you would adopt us
when that time raves from an ambush
that we had not foreseen
and kills us with its arrows

kickapoo burial, remembrance
south of ellsworth

I can tell you
they brought his tobacco
to the clan bundle
then they came back with chanters
and four gourds

they laid him out
at the north end of his house
his feet were to the west
they hung up a blanket
for his dignity

then they washed him
clean cloth and plain water
and combed his hair
and tied it with new ribbon
they fixed an eagle feather
in the crown of the braid

they dressed him in new clothes
painted streaks of purple
from the corners of his eyes
back to his ears
they daubed his moccasins
with that purple
and there was a pinch of tobacco
they folded in each hand

now he could find his own place
at the edge of the other world
he was ready the spirits
would know he was kickapoo

they did not lament him
they thought it would be a bad thing
if anyone did that

parents in the village
blackened the faces of their children
no one would let him
take a child with him

they put him in the grave
east and west
with a spoon and a corn cake
over his heart
and covered him with stone slabs
they told him go with a decent will
into the world of the spirits
and do not harm those who stay here

at sunset
they circled his house with ashes
a ring of fire
so that he could not walk in again
and touch his wife or his children

there was more to it
all that about the clans
but I dont remember
it has been a long time
and more painful than I thought

the grave was just up from the creek
there was a woods there
the settlers used it for camp meetings
later and thats gone too now

two

old settlers day, buckles grove

dollar and a quarter that little
bought an acre of land
peter cartwright marked his way
blazing trees with a hook knife
andrew jackson he was walls freed slave
killed a bloodhound on the ohio bank
thats how he escaped to illinois
he ended up exhorter
you know in the baptist church
there were rolling fires on the prairie
wife rocked the baby in the sugar trough
plough shears were cold-hammered iron
had five yoke of oxen
five board fence on three sides
a thirty-acre plot
set fall door traps for prairie chickens
I danced with the potawatomis
that was before their death march

peter cartwrights dream

monday in my night visions
I thought I went
on a fishing expedition
and I drew up and threw out
many excellent fish

at length I felt that a large fish
or something else
had got hold of my hook
I began to draw whatever it was out
but it came slow and pulled heavy

at length I drew it to land
and behold it was
a large mud turtle
I awoke and lo it was a dream
and I was glad of it

circuit preacher,
lines after cartwright

I just want to say the country
was in an agony of salvation
and I was a lost sheep
bleating around the walls
in a gang by myself

there was an awful shaking
among the dry bones
they waked me up on all sides
and I became
the great deep of a sinner
a heart broken

the devil drank
to a dead hog that day
but I swallowed ezekiel
and tasted his bitter honey

the old hive has sent forth
twenty swarms since then

I wont lean in front of you now
on a broken staff

year of the deep snow

winter of 1830 was the long one
snow in november went into february
four feet deep on the flat
some twenty in the drifts
deer foundered in snowbanks and starved
we dug them out for the hogs
just skinbags of bones
wolves gamboled splayfooted on the crusts
and raided our stock when the deer went
come spring was good times
we rode the wolves down
smashed in their heads with stirrups
I remember one of them
just sat there looking at us
it was the last year we raised any cotton
weather changed I always thought so
grandson says we burnt out the fields
with our bad blue-bellied farming
anyone who got through that winter
they always called him a snowbird

kickapoo dance

there was nothing but prairie
north of blooming grove then
all the way to chicago

they danced in twos
kept time with ankle bells
and the band chief
shaking a gourd full of pebbles

they were smeared with black
and they had these white hands
painted on their chests

old john dawson he danced too
doing their flatfooted steps
but when he thought he could sing with them
the band chief stopped him

he didnt know the words see
hell none of us knew
what it was they were singing

hill prairie

shickshack old winnebago
what did you see here

societies of flowers
shocks of good color
three days ahead of the eye

sunny ridges in prairie shadow
roses in the long valley
yellow daisy purple mint

golden alexander lead plant
chokecherry osage plum
cordgrass maidens tresses

the dream we woke from
before we were ready

three

technology as a spider
webbed in wild roses

gazeteers for a heavenly city
with small copper coins in the roadways
these webs manifest the ineffable quark
that will not be shattered
a fermilab exaltation
amazing almost as a hand
the control room glittering under earth
its plastic christmas tree
aerosol bomb of pine scent
where eyelets are stitched to the hours

these spiders are the sixth order of the angels
they weave here by right
because once in this valley
when earth fell from the skies
they bound it to the stars
now they mould them to the air
these webs commanding our headwaters
they lock them in place forever
deep down complexities
drenched by the red waking sun

clinton

upright cinquefoil there is
a patch of the virgin prairie

and a new kind of storage bin
rising out of the cornfields
but it isnt that at all

chalk message on the bridge
where the creek leads to the cemetery
everybody get high

big wind comes
youre hoping the barn will go down
but it blows down the shed
barn still standing there
like it always was

camelot restaurant and lounge
out of business
windows covered up with plywood
the cooperative feast or famine
experimental corn plot
seems to be thriving however

you can boil water in a fire
or you use a reactor
on a seamless pad of concrete

and these evening primroses
flowers of an hour wild indigo
coralberry pussytoe leaves

625 fuel bundles
columns of uranium dioxide
3500 blades in the steam turbine
950,000 kilowatt generator
pipefitters eden

let us stand with anybody
who stands right
you have to pay attention
to small things
the dead will not be fooled
whatever the time

in the country

1

no buffalo here
1750 the terrible winter
kickapoo reckoning
frozen where they stood

sing jordans stormy bank
come spring my jenny
pick flowers in canaan
on a hill of bones

2

he says if he hums
he can keep her voice cheerful
inside his mind awhile
he always thought of her as a canary
that didnt need any cage for singing

he says he hums now
because everybody interesting
he knows is dead and
nobody alive has anything to say
he wants to listen to

his hair stone white he hums
all the time to himself now
which he did not do
when his wife was alive
she had such a good voice

3

back county musician
he plays for himself
stories the mind covets
songs without words
fragments of old wisdoms

when he grows tired
the valley takes up the silence
and night appears
a soft place
shielding its exiles

now a boy drinks
the death of his father
a girl wears sapphires
in the dollhouse of her dreams
the prophet steps down
any mans pain

follow these directions

go right on 9.75
east to horse creek
at 10.55 the pet paradise cemetery
you can bury your rat there

on the new city road
an abandoned farmhouse
it has three chimneys
cross sangamon south fork
fishing shacks
on the right in the woods

country trail subdivision
sign says it sucks

farm auction

snowflakes they come watching
this rural farewell
farmholders standing in peaked
caps raw hands pocketed
auctioning off blizzards the snow
feathered on the back
screen door and on mirrors a fence slants
farm wife looking down now
staring at a kerchief her face
receding through flurries an unmarked land
winter a sleet in her heart
selling on despair but the snow
prodigal a manna
nobody needs like a swatted fly
or fouled straw steaming on the barn floor
while overhead the fox squirrels
curl under leaves stuffed in autumn
down boles of maple an easy
providence and here is this man
restless with his jars his jugs
vacuum pumps bales of alfalfa
tractors faces of dead snowflakes
going for sandwiches chili hot coffee
somewhere in the city the white
city where the snow waits

decatur

baroque towers of millikins old main
dna stretch of eldorado that drag
franchised as they are these days
and pershing old black jack
parallel and as bedight
this town surprises you
town leading into doors
that may or may not be opened
like a work of mahler
with a heart wounded in it

streets of sweat and yearning
they make everything in this
steam crowned city all these
air bearing crankshaft casings
easy ice cream scoops cardboard containers
made by hands laced with razor cuts
pasteurized ice milk and pumps and
imitation bacon bits who can say
from imitation hogs and corn sweeteners
and gear case housings stove knob inlays
creeper wheel assemblies potato chips
so many things here this very thingness
smolders in the whorls of our fingers
carburetor valve seats concentrate
vinyl and fabric cleaner
neatsfoot compound one hundred percent
natural diaper sweet blue raindrops
spider dance centipede hiphooray kites
laboring in the corridors of the air

saint johns lutheran cemetery
northeast of town
it is a verdant place
tertocha schalbe semelka karasch
schudzara brix tanzyus artz
hungarians and lithuanians
meat cutters and produce packers
sleep here among many friends
and south along this green rectangle
a siding for robin egg blue tank cars
track old and waffled
it cant last long

this town has tomatoes born for the future
that hydroponic renewal
freight cars assembled by computer
and there are golf courses a swimming pool
lake activities prospects
a ymca a good downtown library
junior college etcetera

hard business and hardball times
would that work could sweep us into heaven
rising in a chemical yeast
these old saints they want to come home
walk through an open door
as a man might enter a woman
all in his hallowed bones as if she knew
or could know who he was

four

lunch room, new berlin

I told him he needed
his head trimmed a shadow
he said why he was
the hometown bald eagle
where he came from
I wouldnt have believed him
what with his chinwhiskers
drizzling into his soupbowl
why he said last graduation
the superintendent of schools in his town
tripped on his own beard and broke
both ankles and now
the old timers drinking coffee
round back of the pharmacy
drape their beards on his crutches
keep them out of the cigarette butts
and stuff on the floor that way
I thought I would be polite
just give him a vague nod
but he went right at it
said anyone needed a haircut
where he lived they had to
lift up the barbers eyebrows
see if he was awake or just
standing at the window like a rock
I didnt believe that either
but he just jellied up a bun
and went on expostulating
told me where he came from
nobody went to the cemetery
but it wasnt like oklahoma
where those wheat farmers
are so lean and dehyderated
they use them for fence posts

when they die that is
except for the ones the woodpeckers get
no sir he told me
everyone is heavy in the haunch
back there in monticello
great chested good sound smiling folks
with hair all over them like pelts
when someone dies in monticello
they put him out in the yard
you can always tell which ones is shrubs
because no family lets a starling
sit in a relative
I humored him of course
because we were having lunch together
but when he wanted to know
would I like one of his hushpuppies
I said I surely would not
if it wasnt a chihuahua
I got him with that one
parted him right up the middle
when I said that dont you think

self made in bloomington

the big insurance executive
heh heh has been retired
now what does he care ha ha ha
for institutional liquidity
he says that a dozen firemen
are worth ten hundred executives
points out how thoughtful they are
passing through hospital zones
with muffled sirens and bells

he goes around the house
with his musical comb now
plays oh susanna to the end
and again to the end
truly the artist
although the tissue paper
bothers his nose some

his wife cringes in the playroom
hiding in earphones and offenbach
thinks if she marries again
lord send her a man
with sense and a perfect pitch
or at least one with the head bald

watching a haircut

they dont put you down
six feet anymore
just forty-two inches
say thats enough now
why its hardly below frost
well they say you cant heave out
the vaults a ton and a half
and what about the water table
how about we get rain for a month
I ask them that and they say
well one did rise up
on polecat creek near chatham
last year first of march
but they was an admiral in it
so it was all right

talent show

the all girl kazoo band
the wives mothers singles
they are dressed in white formals
and wear blue sashes

they dont mind very much
whether or not they play well
just so long as they know
they all look beautiful

isnt that delicious

one of the girls
eases herself over to me
she reaches into her bodice
with both hands
and pulls out two kazoos

she says see I have two kazoos
and I say oh well ah why yes
you really do
have two kazoos

concert at normal

these six triangle players
they are all hanging beards
george bingham would have grappled them
for his flatboats
or put them in the stump speaker
watching a dogfight

they should have been border raiders
riding high on their high
thudding horses
rousing it up in northwest missouri
over autumn hypnotic dirt lanes
sprung wild with marijuana

but these young musicians
are six students
from illinois state university
it is theater that counts with them
and finesse
they know you cant be aggressive
with triangles

therefore beneath those globes of silence
the ingenuous stars
they ping and ping and ping
ping ping and ping

bulldog crossing

you want to get to kincaid
you drive down this road
turn west just before taylorville
you pass the dump on your left then
reach kincaid at the river
or east of it I guess

well this place does have a strange name
used to be a lot of bulldogs here
a hundred or more bulldogs
that was before the stock market crashed

they liked to sit where we are now
watching the trucks go south
trucks was new then and the road
had good pavers I think

it was something to see those dogs
with pie-pan muzzles and cropped ears
homing like magnets
whenever a truck went by

but I tell you the truth
those dogs were just like people
some days they just got tired
sitting on this side the road
and then they would all stand up
and go over to the other side

used to be a big cottonwood there
and they liked to sit in its shadow
watching the trucks roll north
must have been halfway to decatur

so you understand how it was
them going back and forth and forth and back
bulldog crossing just naturally
came to be called this place

well no the dogs are all gone now
they were all overcome by ambition
everyone of them ran for election
and they all burst forth
with healthy pluralities
as edmund burke would put it

why they made three governors
and sixty-five congressmen those were
truly honorable dogs and there were
several got on the supreme court and some
were senators and foreign ambassadors

you could say they were the best
politicians for bulldogs there ever were
except for the one was a complainer
he never went any place
but he had a flea in his ear
about something

you want to know about him
he went into writing wrote this book
portrait of the young dog as an artist
won a big prize hey wait I want to tell you
they made it a movie
john wayne had a part in it

five

old name old river

mowawequa the old name
for this old river
face of the wolf
has it over south fork
has it in this water
sun in a dapple toward
light in shimmers and they
reaching infinity and then
a calm moon rising
with its long cradling
vowels of light

one time at sangchris
there were white deer
they trembled at the rivers edge
frail and luminous
beneath a wash of stars
or in some eclipse
feeding on their own light
an imagination of shadows
lost in a slow river
with its choiring of wolves

another nile for pharaoh

1

big town for its size
the river bleeding to death I am
astonished the chubs
leaping at the bank for dear life
red water murky it takes
a paper mill to do this
an international corporation
of chub killers
I look up the sky
seems so pure what the hell

2

underneath the bridge
a refrigerator with its new
door gaping pickle jar
tilted on the shelf

and caught in driftwood
downstream from a quiet pool
black plastic bags
stuffed with someones dead dreams

south fork sunday

the peoples bank of rosamund is closed
greek revival empty another god dead
two burnt-out trucks side by side in a quarry
one mans tax write-off
another mans depression
they are loaded with chat
but they wont be going anywhere

the town of ohlman
wakes up dawn come sunday
everybody goes to church
or sits in the side yards on lawn chairs
or a family paints the doghouse
worth talking about a month of sundays

graffiti on the tin outhouse wall
god rides a harley
government without justice is a ripoff
someone reading his augustine

this is where the south fork rises
deep in christian county
welling through bronze cornets
hindemiths brass
the long fanfare of trumpet vine

fisher woods in spring

here are some wild flowers
spring beauties on the sangamon
so formal at the cotillion
all white satins and pinks
awkward modesties
vulnerable to smiles

their younger sisters the bluebells
saucy in petticoats would rather roll hoops

and suddenly lonesome in these deep woods
dogtooth violets
those mother superiors
the dance getting on without them
bowing down to their prayers

lick creek my own branch

idyllic in the afternoon
flattened with a clayey jet soil
silting through woods
from the cornfield up higher
branch defined sharply
deer tracks at angles
and the ubiquitous raccoon
signing a dark outing
and all in a fright suddenly
the heavy print here
it must have been german shepherd
green-eyed and nervous midnight
the gray wolf running in him

I look for shagbark
you can boil the chips
three hours drain off the water
and simmer that three hours
with brown sugar
down soft to a syrup
appalachian and sweet
but the aftertaste is bitter
the hickory wanton in it
I have no luck so turn to home
my footprint in this place
with the deer the dog the raccoon
and the silt that levels them

rain and more rain

1

the bees have given up
too much for them
no sun rising nectar
the honey in reserve is gone
they are almost to the queens
they have cut across the hives
devoured their own larvae
beekeepers in pawnee and divernon
stay them with sugar water

april rain and rain through june
the unsignatured fields
more emerald than pictures of ireland
flowerless as the sahara
and on the compost heaps
the squash luminous with blossoms
engulfed cathedrals
that will not set fruit

the wine makers of thayer
drift their grape with elderberry
perhaps not this year

2

rainwater pouring down sugar creek
roiling with silt
pouring from the cornfields
those old runs rills branches creeks
tiled under the prairies
they are out again

this all day fourth of july rain
has pitched them full flood
the whole landscape articulate

soundings in glacial drift

1

there is a fifty-foot drop
from the shelbyville moraine
it is something so gentle
you cannot believe it
then the illinois till plain
rolls the horizon west before you
a flat miracle that defeats the eye

at the county line road
the macon and christian county divide
there is a benchmark
copper green on a culvert wall
it is precisioned
at the intersected baseline
of the third principal meridian
this is the interior of our interior
pending from the numeraled stars

south of this place
through walls of dust
you can see glacial kames
sucked from wisconsin meltdowns
the ice two miles high then
think of it

2

fields black dead grass
along the edge of the road
silver machine shed big still windmill
a blue sky and black trees
a new bridge in a level valley
fishermen coming from there

down the cerro gordo-cisco road

on the curve out of la place
no moraines here it is flat like auburn
there is a round water tower
and small tourist cabins set there in the thirties

cerro gordo with crumbling red brick
buds hac sump pump special
farmers branch building 1887
a great house on the edge of town
there is always one
with aging black cypresses around it
mansion going down to seed

cisco is all crossroads
and grain bins and silos
you look straight up to see them
define the clouds
la avenida de las grain elevators
the kids buy cokes at the antique store
you can get cartons of milk at the gas station
no one wastes land here
on anything but crops

3

william j bryan the gold cross
who can afford it
only russians and south africans

here in this town north of 72
the methodist church
has a cross of split rails

split black locust
ancient and weathered
and poor as the town

I think the congregation
would tolerate
a presbyterian on it

4

there is a very fine
pleistocene outwash
fronting tom lincolns place
the sangamon gouges that bluff
with every spring raise
but summers you can walk below it
and pick up stones streaked with copper
or maybe a saucer rim
chinese version
with english castles
you wonder who sipped his coffee
cool from it and when that was

valentines day

that slant in the west sun
trapping blue shadows in wind riffs
sweet day that brightens the eye
like a quick thank-you note
small envelopes in the mailbox
birds mated on this day
feathering in cathedral niches
the girl down the street
came up pregnant her family
rejoiced the thought of a grandchild
the boyfriend was thirteen
there will be honey in his gallstones
I print in the heart on a card
I love you where are you

mano

this stone the life in it
the man who shaped it
trusting his own culture
walking the continent
simply at home
this essential implement these edges
indented sides disturbed
already restless in the dust of those
suns he was made of
a form the possibility
that cracked leg bones for marrow
a maul or a grinder for seeds
earlier than the angels this
figure breathing his light

fter sundown

e rabbi breathes slowly
d house slippers
lden in the dark
says the man who digs his own grave
s a hole in the pit of the world
says we are far from shore
matter we know
open waters of the ocean
an hurrying like a rumor
ot be a three-dimensional figure
st a cool light
op to draw water
someone begs him for rain

owl in the

something r
a resurgenc
took him a

the incred
walks the
nowhere

he says i
everyon

the jud
thinks
they c

old state capitol

good woodwork walnut
spindles in the stairwells
a comfortable restoration
place like a man
taking it easy

moment fixed a legislature
adjourned an old top hat
upside down on a desk
trials and debates at an end
some eternal solstice

here was a haunt for lawyers
logan and oglesby
davis trumbull little douglas
grant down from galena in the war
and lincoln who would
lie in state here one day
hard to believe now

so the wise children
visit this place of a morning
they have this
intimate thing they do
crowning the oak dowels
in the plank floor with pennies

lincoln tomb, a report

husband to wife with camera
can you get the whole tomb
no she says from the viewfinder
but Ive got mr lincoln I think

—a terrorist got him
rendered him to an insane absolute
one of our martyred presidents—

the gutzon borglum sculpture
the same on mount rushmore
robert todd marveled at it
he did not expect to see father again

husband focuses on wife
she rubs the borglum nose
a grandfather lifts two children
a small boy and his sister
it is the custom that everyone
shines mr lincolns nose

I sit on a park bench
watch the people gathering
always the families and foreign groups
the busloads of old tourists
and now a sun-bronzed woman
the nudists call a cottontail
her white behind
peeking from under her shorts
as she strolls to the tomb

palace for pharaoh
hedges of solemn yew
and burning bush

and a dogwood on each side of the entrance
camped there for blossoms in spring
no arch here
just the necessary
post and lintel

many languages spoken
I recognize spanish italian chinese
but there are others
the world cares about this man
comes here to have its picture taken
each family its several selves
poses for a group portrait
this is essential in front of the tomb
like rubbing the polished nose

while deep within
the cenotaph spells his name
and those numbers 1809–1865

a small son to his father
I saw that I saw that
was he in back of that thing

—yes ten and a half feet
behind the dark red arkansas stone
and ten feet down
safe under tons of cement

it is all right this tomb
his words hung in bronze here
gettysburg address
farewell to springfield
second inaugural the almighty

has his own purposes
blood drawn with a lash
every drop paid with a sword

I expect it to wear as well
as any thing I have produced
a truth I thought needed to be told

this terrible war
if god wills it to continue

from the side at a distance
the borglum sculpture seems enormous
a head on a judgment seat
some thing in front of the gate
we need to dare touch
it tells us who we are isnt that right
or should have been
or who we have to be

father impatient with his son
you ask me questions
I dont have any idea
how to answer

a teenage boy exits the tomb
he is alone approaching the sculpture
he rubs it vigorously
taking his solitary good-by
no magic here or sanctioned custom
his is the last fierce
affectionate touch
we reserve for the dead

and now a small child
walking to the parking lot
stops in the sunlight
she is wearing a red beanie
which supports a plastic propeller
she studies for a moment the shadow
that revolves above her shadow
and then goes on

snowflakes and recorders

lindsays house on a cold
sunday afternoon
in springfield
table laid with his service
reception sweet punch and cookies
I am disappointed my ankles freezing
but the recorder trio seems
impervious to the cold
they warm to their renaissance concert
they play an unnamed song
by king henry the eighth
and it is beautiful

this house has so many histories
lindsay his birth and death here
lincoln his sister-in-laws house
his last night in springfield here
so much of hope in these rooms
poems and political memories

snow a few flakes outside the window
fireplace needs a damper or a screen
henry the eighth this afternoon
sovereign of a clutch of talent
a crude power that took down
it seems only the best of men
and now his song
lovely and a surprise

vachel we dont know
what to do with our lives
how fill them up
how not even to be self conscious
our successes squeezed from us

despite our failings and yet
there are some like figures
on a cave wall
and when we find them
they teach us and we change

presidential election with
blackbirds and swallows

rain drying in the fields
swallows on top of things like aldermen
the more analyses in the papers
the sicker the elections look
but what should I say
I cant slot a ballot without help
so how could I run the country
the flag is limp at the polling place
blackbirds are whistling
behind it in the woods
black diamonds mating
why this might help everyone
an achievement of mutual objectives
I want to express my appreciation
the selflessness of these birds
their contribution to my candidacy
not knowing how the vote would go

ice is a thin rim on the lake
it will be gone come friday
winter devalued at last and with it
the issues outstanding
nevertheless you should watch yourself
they have these three baskets the third
has the shrunken head you open
that one and death pops a weasel
how difficult these responsibilities
pent up in democracy who votes who doesnt
the chances you take
if candor is the voice of the nation
the office vanishing in the white
brilliance of the orator

you want to hear one voice
shake a government down
morning into night the terrible grief

seven

ww II veteran

I remember the boxcars
there was one full of legs
and another just had the arms
and one had the lopped off bodies
and a fourth was crammed with heads

it doesnt take the same heat to burn an arm up
as it does a torso you understand that

there were some camp guards
who surrendered but I dont know
whatever became of them
they must have been thrown somewhere

funny how it works
I had a cousin fought in the pacific
he knocked out teeth
made himself a necklace of gold fillings
he died a week ago last sunday

beneath the clocks at mason city
thinking of the neutron bomb

1

concrete twelve feet
lead six feet
banked earth ten feet
the internal hemorrhage
the seven day dying
the twenty year silence

the banded roach
the mouse that comes
to its death in winter
measure that silence

2

rabbit without a foot
stunned in the moonlight

where we came from and dangerous
the house uneasy
its evidence of talent

cities in flat dimensions
nurseries even empty of love

another universe adrift
the static entering ours

who would miss us

lines for the tribe of ben ishmael

bound in sheaves
nebeker dalama basore

gone to detroit and chicago
gone to philadelphia
gone to earth

all held all sealed in the last
dream of the pomegranate
cambodians vietnamese
russians armenians biafrans
dutchman and greek gypsy jew
the rorschach for all the others

and that was 1908 in indiana
the year that could not be trammeled
in its own time
for rapists imbeciles idiots
let there be surgeons
when procreation is inadvisable

as the law came down
like a blot on foolscap
they clustered in the arbors of frost
and the night danced until dawn
for them and their children

carters of wood
or wash or whatever
and their orphaned daughters
who told the fierce stories
and those beggars in the streets
who wore no robes of green silk
or golden bracelets

the dangerous blind old men
who mocked their eyes
with blue vitriol

they were the sober hunters
gamel melamnhe hamella
anchoring their shanties
on the white river mudflats
they did not search for paradise
or dream of it even
because they knew
god was not there
walking the hedgerows
in that walled garden

churry aimen hayar
they went once each year
northwest through morocco
then summered by mahomet
and fall edging winter
crossed back east over the wabash
where mecca is
and on to indianapolis

they had tecumsehs blessing
before he went to the dead
these thousand years

memorial day camp butler

time to commemorate
the national dead
time for the triple bright flag
the regimental banners
time for the tears
the serious faces
time for the trumpeter
and the echoing trumpeter
time for saying the wrong things
time for the dead to forgive us

eight

man looking for his wife

you have a rough skin have you
seen the girl in the red cape
the one I married so long ago
I will always shout for her she was
my cookie my damp noodle my bread pudding
she will escape the pit surely
my longing will lift her up safely
my cuddled bunny my button she was
the sweet chocolate that iced my gold cake
my sugared butter my ghat my stranger
my yearning my unspanked virginity
gardens encompassed protected by angels
I grinned in my toothpaste
over the steam in my bathroom mirror
I sang on the bedroom door
with the knobby choirs of my knuckles
me the good irish bricklayer
my polished shillelagh tucked neatly
under my armpit I came into her
my reciprocal duty my honor
my fish and chip all in her raging
breaking up millstones I was so faithful
my delicious potato dumpling
I want to roll her up in a ball
tuck her away in my knapsack
she was so clean so washed so bright
the one who bit me when I was not looking
the rose hip who stamped my eyes red
my mouth my jaw the spider on my cheek
the one who struck me rang me
tied me in knots kneaded me knitted me
came unto me like the dark knife
that stunned a half death in my soul
my mud dauber my market my perch on a gallows

the knack who burred and honed my weakness
who ascended the strong tower of my frailty
oh poor bleak heart and hair belly
I look for her with every sundown
wandering the broken prisms of my senses

man in overalls

north of pleasant plains
all my life
anyone can tell you
charlie is my name well
you get old the barn is a place
and catfood keeps in a tin
will do as well as a roast and
it doesnt cost so much
see you go off after so many years
healthy or not
so next fall I climb to the loft
and when spring comes
they can look for me in that place
I dont complain whats fair
whats unfair my life was
only a little life
but you can tell everybody
I did not end it myself

some damn odin
eats us up dont you think
one by one by one
he holds us upside down
by our ankles and what
can we do with him
nothing I can tell you

my mother died in let me see
that was in the thirties she had
a green disposition
she always thought of me
as her sorrow
I gave her the toothache she always said
I was like someone in an old coat

with stars and a moon on it
what could she do with me
I think of her once in a while

god he has an eye
that responds to dim light
there are hot-eyed angels
windowed in cartwrights church
and gods mother
looks angry as a miners bride
down there in saint benedicts
judgment and insurrection
angels and all women
it dont pay sleeping in church
something is sure to slip by you

my mothers face
she mirrored a smile she thieved
from some busy forgetfulness
well the wheat goes down anyway
smoke of the harvest so pungent
I would tell her the world
had wonders so many miracles
those sacred waters
dont think that will free you
she would answer with a bang
I think of this
after so long a time
wiping my eyes
with the tips of my fingers
I was always the first day
of the year with her
I was never a match for her

our cells break down
they blow piffs of excitement
clasping their little knees
while their bellies shake
like pots and pans
hanging on the kitchen wall
an odd collection

listen to me for one moment
so you will remember it
there are 220,000 rods in the retina
of a guinea pigs eye
guinea pigs do not have visible tails
and they are used for experiments
like men without hope
and that is as many miles to the moon
as many soldiers saved at dunkirk
well think about this
and think how many rods in jehovahs eye
how many bound in the unblinking eye of yahweh
those rods are the murdered of this earth
where gods eye opens and closes
they are the legions of the murdered dead
and their murderers
I tell you they drown in the blind
universe of gods own eye
clutching at oars

here you want my photograph
it is full of empty spaces
I dont complain
we are all in a net
the brutes that kill us
are more than the galaxies

we love the law
like madmen love their skins
I say my prayers
jack be nimble jack will you light
my candlewick I want to
snuff it out with 220,000 tears

well this is a little song
my mother taught me
evenings during the depression
you can sing it for me
when they find the cap and overalls
and my bones in the loft next spring
please pardon me
the old man said
but Im so hungry
I think Im dead

salt creek, kickapoo
winter story

1

we were in the fourth world
the one destroyed by fire

the thunderers
brooded on those who were evil
kept them in their hutches
but the horned panthers
rose at the worlds end anyway
and devoured us all

the thunderers vanished
even the horned panthers
and all those who had names
who attended the night dances

2

this was the dirt world
scraped off the flippers
of the snapping turtle

we gambled two male turtles
and seven female
and we lost every one of them
then we gambled the dead turtle
sprawled in moonlight on the highway

the world is a carapace
falling through space end over end
a rattle with a hole in it

3

no gold now no winning
all that melted down
hidden under loess
america of ten thousand years
taking its own back
all gone golden and gold

prophet with radiant eyes
prophet blind in his bones
dancing and dancing at the ark
sweet inebriate prophet
drunk in the tears of christ
our long still night

old priest and his blessing

this is a year
with a soft sound
a monteverdi time it will have life
a good vivaldi you will have
this decade for your own anthems
it will not disappear with me
it will be only
my perceptions
that I draw down with me

my voice in its whisper
where time is unthinkable
country life so exalted
with bagpipes and hurdy-gurdies
wide ranging dances
purcell and the kings instruments
baroque theater of christs navel
those nuclear movements
puppet show with hand dolls
their heads shining

bow your head
bow down your head
these hands in the ancient lost
pulse beat of their dying
will bless you in moments
keyed to chopin
they wish you the exquisite chance
all that persistence
when duration is nothing
as the auditorium darkens
and the silence fills us

a cool asperges and censers
here are my hands
elevated from this
bed of pain
magnificats dressed in their
battle regalia

nine

sandalwood poems

1

always in your loving
there is so much sorrow
there is the wind
uncertain in the crowns
of summer maple
there is the everlasting
conciliation of the tides

2

I offer you
ten meadows of fireflies

you give me
one box of sandalwood

3

I circle this table
I do not come back to the place
where I began
though I want to
say that I do

perhaps you are the one
who is constant really
a red warning light
that never changes

I want to go a long way
where I will find myself
not as in a mirror
but as that other man who comes

from the other side of time
who will merge with my spirit
and achieve my body

I will wear him
laughing when I return to you
coming back to the old place
that was not mine

4

house wind sleep

we do not raise
our voices

you hand me down
my body

princess candidate,
sangamon county fair

thank you for listening to me
but I must tell you
I am not native to this county
because I was conceived
far east of broadwell in indiana
my parents coming to williamsville
shortly after and I
was born there and that was
five summers ago last june 21st

and that is how it is
I am the gnawed bone of my
fathers desire the starlight
of my mothers dreaming
I am the bean blossom of their
happy needfulness
my mother luxuriously yawning
oh you were wonderful
and my father his face shining
like an apple you duck for
in the kitchen on halloween
did you really think so

I am in other respects
like everyone here
I am starred with bethlehem
I will have my crown of thorns
but there will be
hosannas too in my life
and delectable mountains
as in everyones life

I can do hots
I like jacks on a rainy day
I can skip to blue heaven
following a stone
and sometimes I bake saucies
for my girlfriends
and saturdays when the house is quiet
I like all the cartoons

but to be spellbound
that is special
that is when the tv news
calls us to lives
where everything is lost
and people stand
somewhere else in their shadows
and they win over cruelty
as adlai stevenson said
in the courage of their fortitude
that is when no one can wrap them in packages
or sell them anymore
it puts a stitch in my heart
seeing them like that
those good prairie people
facing what is beyond them
in every direction

oh but forgive me prattling
and let me turn for you
like a shaker in kentucky
so you can see me all around
and please accept this curtsy
and my smile to you good-by

late winter in menard county

1

new salem in patches of snow
I see how the culture
spoke in its hand tools
smooth curves of grain cradles
handles in good polish
for apple butter paddles
and things of strict importance
flails reap hooks tarbuckets

then there are the fabrics
those subtle colors
native elderberry and walnut
subdued horizons of goldenrod
woven after patience
that must have been godly
with flax hackles teasels
drop spindles

and the quilts and spreads
their thimbled excellence
stitchery that explained the years
bear paw maple leaf ohio star
abstractions of secret hands

2

well everybody in petersburg
got out of the house by eleven
they turned up at the middle school
where the kiwanis
had a pancake and sausage day
people were tired of winter
like braid rugs slung over porch rails

politics in the cafeteria
hello Im running for supreme court
how are you today
not bad for a gentile
are you related to the state senator
I am the state senator

3

edgar lee masters your town
has a new day-care center
it is going up on the back rear wall
of mentor grahams old house
you must have known it the one
with the port wine brick
and the clumsy gingerbread
holding up so well for a teachers digs

your house is public now
and visitors can see the scratched table
where you wrote your proscriptions
for country graveyards

the town made you a fine afternoon
for your centennial did you know that
the school band in the gymnasium
played vaguely through several
variations and there were
pretty good speeches
and a commemorative stamp

4

this is a late winter river
a dangerous sangamon
with a jerry-built dam

the awkward angle rebuffs the current
it backs in an eddy
below the west bank
and small whirlpools
surface and disappear in it
like mouths in a pit
an insidious babble
whispering in a sick mans soul

it was the weekend after taxes
as people remember
when kevin washington
lost his life here with the child
he tried to save lifted on his arm
so it was mid april
all in a swollen spring

the whole town knows
the sangamon is a living current
that does not abide still water

so some here will tell you
the river sucked him down
and evened a score with his grandfather
who snatched so many from the river

bath

and when lincoln came here
that was august 16th 1858
he felt like his age was something
hanging on him he remembered
surveying the town 22 years earlier
in deep wilderness then and river timber
how he staked out the first plat
with his own hands he said

and these old men around him
they were as young as himself
27 years ago in 1831
messmates in the black hawk war

the crowd heard him with respect
tell all of them why slavery
was an evil thing

bath is trailers and shacks
and make-do livings anyway you can
full of particular folk
who like pink flamingos in driveways
and peonies on the lawns
cradled in used tractor tires
things good for looking at
they tell you if you want to know

lincoln had six years
beyond his stump speech at bath
six years for the history of the world

this year in late spring
the children will go down the river bank
midmorning on memorial day

as they have since the civil war
and set their little boats
drifting on the illinois
with cargoes of flowers

poem for scott lucas

1

crisp weather on sand ridge prairie
british soldiers those reciprocations
deep in the winter dry grass
bright dots of red in bright green moss
small yuletides on a lowering day

blackjack oak on sandy hillocks
a pair of blue shotgun shells in the blackjack
scrub oak rare in illinois
whirr of a chainsaw where it doesnt belong
teenagers working from a pickup

2

cass and mason counties
with their straight ditches
names like tazewell and red oak or allens grove
and small towns hard to come by
teheran and goofy ridge and san jose
and chandlerville beneath the levee
where someone used to go to the dances
and those old illinois ports
beardstown and havana
where one duck may have to quack twice now
not like the old seasons scott
when they clamored the skies shut
but the long delicate raincats
they coax the soil up rich again
a honeymouthed eurydice
fields heaved out in rows by the mile
with melons an autumn moon cries over
these two counties work us down
the good hours and even hands

one more generous harvest
once again for a little while

3

that pilot of a mud river west
comes rapping his chains
slipping cleats with those long
deck clanking loops so easy for him
tobacco chunked in his jaw like a bitt
he leaning on a shrieking whistle
as if anyone would challenge
right of way with so formidable a riverman
red coals piercing his spider eyes
hair slithering in black tangles
his shoulders groaning under scales
green with decay from a dead river

pray god a man might turn out his pocket
a roosevelt dime or a good worn penny
when the blast of that pilots whistle
jerks the dead loose from their dreams
on the far bank of that other world

primroses and meadowlark eggs

they come from their
timeless periods the indian
paintbrush the plaintain in a monthly
halo where no voice
has been lost in the western
maytime of dropseed
and meadowlark eggs

hidden in the brave wind
larkspur wild strawberry
a voice talking in the womb
of the primrose a catalogue
of ravaging

sweetheart the box
terrapin the regal fritillary
blues that distill the eye
you are drawn through these veins
so natural the cottonwoods
echo in the wind the voice
saying who you are

all shadows pale greens
the sharp reds in spangles

confluence

the suns eye gleams on the burnt black prairie
the winter blackened moraines of all conclusions
and the white egret
ascetic alone with his promise
knowing where the river is
threads a fiery needle

it was always more than dawn
that we looked for
something that we had not seen
as we watched here
gathered from the ashes of our vision

may new prayers and new fires
the beloved pleiades
welcome the kickapoo home
star daughters in their hoods of light
dancing at their zenith while the sun
burns down the horizon

this world in peace
this laced temple of darkening colors
it could not have been made for shambles
this green twilight of echoing voices
as the sun hurls its fireball
down the other side of the world

it is long miles through marshgrass
the sangamon sifting to its ending
and beyond us the illinois
intensifies south
beneath the eagles at grafton
our ancient mississippi
its wide slow waters

notes

marquette in winter camp

In ill health, the Jesuit explorer had to wait out the cold months before going on to establish a mission among the Illinois tribes. The letter was written to his superior, Father Henri Nouvel. Marquette did preach to the Illinois in April 1675, but died a month later on the return journey to the home mission of Saint Ignace in the upper Great Lakes.

beneath our tamaroa starlight

The Tamaroa were members of the Illinois confederacy, which included the Kaskaskia, Moingwena, Michigamea, Peoria, and the Cahokia. The Tamaroa were virtually destroyed by an Iroquois war party at the confluence of the Illinois and Mississippi rivers in 1680. The remnant is thought to have merged with the Cahokia, and so vanished from history as a distinctive people. The Tamaroa were the Sangamon valley hunters and gatherers.

tamaroa prayer

An extant vocabulary list for the Illinois and Miami gives French and native terms and a bilingual rendering of the Lord's Prayer. Assuming that the Tamaroa were acquainted with this prayer, this is how they might have understood it.

kickapoo burial

The Kickapoo moved from the Great Lakes after the decline of the Tamaroa and settled in Indiana and eastern and central Illinois. They established villages from the mouth of the Sangamon at present-day Beardstown to its source at Ellsworth. A hard-fighting and independent nation, one band settled in Coahuila, Mexico, in the 1860s. This group relocated in Texas in 1982, and in 1985 purchased a tract of good farmland along the Rio Grande.

peter cartwrights dream

A Methodist preacher and circuit rider, he spent years evangelizing the western country of Illinois. He came to the Sangamon valley in 1823 and established his church in Pleasant Plains.

hill prairie

Shickshack, a Winnebago band chief, had a village several miles west of Petersburg in the Sangamon valley. He is said to have removed to Wisconsin in 1827. His followers are thought to have encouraged Black Hawk to surrender. Shickshack's Knob, between Opossum Hollow and Fancher Creek, commemorates his presence on the Sangamon. Shickshack liked to sit up there on summer nights, avoiding the heat and mosquitoes in the valley below. Early settlers often joined him on the hill.

technology as a spider webbed in wild roses

Spiders are creatures of special power for the Kickapoo. Earth, sun, and moon are held together in the web of a great spider.

old name old river

Sangchris is the name for a state park which straddles the borders of Sangamon and Christian counties. White deer are occasionally reported among the herd there.

soundings in glacial drift

William Jennings Bryan, subject of a spirited poem by Lindsay, tireless standard-bearer for the Democratic party and father to the compassionate tradition in contemporary politics, was a graduate of Illinois College in Jacksonville.

lines for the tribe of ben ishmael

The Ishmaelites are spoken of in Fenimore Cooper's *The Prairie*. A people with a cohesive and perhaps Muslim identity, they appear to have descended from escaped slaves, runaway bond servants, and remnant Native American groups. James Whitcomb Riley's "Little Orphant Annie" may have been a Ben Ishmaelite girl.

poem for scott lucas

Scott W. Lucas of Havana was majority leader in the U.S. Senate during the Truman administration. He led the fight in the Senate for approval of the North American Treaty Organization, funding for the Marshall Plan, and appropriations for Truman's Point Four Program.

POETRY FROM ILLINOIS

History Is Your Own Heartbeat
Michael S. Harper (1971)

The Foreclosure
Richard Emil Braun (1972)

The Scrawny Sonnets and
Other Narratives
Robert Bagg (1973)

The Creation Frame
Phyllis Thompson (1973)

To All Appearances: Poems New
and Selected
Josephine Miles (1974)

Nightmare Begins Responsibility
Michael S. Harper (1975)

The Black Hawk Songs
Michael Borich (1975)

The Wichita Poems
Michael Van Walleghen (1975)

Cumberland Station
Dave Smith (1977)

Tracking
Virginia R. Terris (1977)

Poems of the Two Worlds
Frederick Morgan (1977)

Images of Kin: New and
Selected Poems
Michael S. Harper (1977)

On Earth as It Is
Dan Masterson (1978)

Riversongs
Michael Anania (1978)

Goshawk, Antelope
Dave Smith (1979)

Death Mother and Other Poems
Frederick Morgan (1979)

Local Men
James Whitehead (1979)

Coming to Terms
Josephine Miles (1979)

Searching the Drowned Man
Sydney Lea (1980)

With Akhmatova at the
Black Gates
Stephen Berg (1981)

More Trouble with the Obvious
Michael Van Walleghen (1981)

Dream Flights
Dave Smith (1981)

The American Book of the Dead
Jim Barnes (1982)

Northbook
Frederick Morgan (1982)

The Floating Candles
Sydney Lea (1982)

Collected Poems, 1930–83
Josephine Miles (1983)

The River Painter
Emily Grosholz (1984)

The Passion of the
Right-Angled Man
T. R. Hummer (1984)

Eroding Witness
Nathaniel Mackey (1985)

Poems from the Sangamon
John Knoepfle (1985)